1. Introduction

"Greetings! This is Philip the photographer. I'm on my way to your home and will be there in about 30 minutes!"

While I usually go by Phil, this is the text message that I send several times a day to realtors and homeowners to let them know I'm en-route to them. I use text to talk on my phone as much as possible when driving. Despite my phones' familiarity with my voice and speech patterns, when I say Phil, it will write "fill." Sometimes when I say Philip it will read "fill up." So, then I spend my time in the car correcting the message, creating an even more dangerous driving experience…you have to love technology!

My name is Phil and I am a real estate photographer. I actually began my journey in the real estate industry in the year 2000, right after graduating high school. From being a full-time agent, to working on real estate teams, to processing short sales and working as an office administrator, I have been involved in every aspect of real estate. Somehow, I landed in full time photography, drone operation, and videography. Since I was a child, my love has been for music and anything else that allowed me to be creative. So, when I was introduced to the concept of photography as used in real estate in 2010, I was completely intrigued.

That year, I was working as a listing coordinator and glorified receptionist for Coldwell Banker in Tampa, FL. I loved the agents and staff that I worked with, but the pay was bad and the room for long term growth was limited. Plus, it wasn't very interesting, and I was bored out of my mind. I felt like I was in Groundhog Day with Bill Murray. In fact, I even wrote a song about it (shameless plug — it's on one of my YouTube channels).

Looking for a way to supplement my income, I found a job writing real estate descriptions on Fiverr.com. The person posting the job was also named Phil and we struck up a relationship immediately. One day I noticed the signature line of his email said, "real estate photographer." I asked him if he could tell me more about that and…the rest is history. My life changed the day I met Phil. In fact, I dedicate this book to him because he changed my life and has inspired me to do the same for others. I came to the table with a great amount of experience in this field but he introduced me to a whole different aspect. Once I realized it existed, it just clicked! The knowledge and experience he shared with me has been a gift, almost like a superhero ability. To this day we remain very close friends. I want to share this gift with as many other people as possible.

Since high school, I have always been searching for additional income streams. MLMs were very attractive to me, even selling weird stuff (I sold knives door to door) — just anything that's kinda out of the box. I am extremely gullible, too. I'll believe whatever sales pitch is given me and tell myself, "I can do that!" Up until this point, nothing I tried really worked. I've wasted a ton of time and money just trying to find ways to make money. But I am very excited and proud to say that real estate photography worked for me! I can also assure you that I came into this with ZERO photography experience. To this day, I will not claim to be a high-tech guru or gearhead or extremely knowledgeable about the inner workings of photography. I am none of these things. But what I have been taught has given me all the tools needed to succeed in this job.

Which leads me to a question…what is success?

I think it's something different for everyone. But for me, it meant having a job that I enjoyed, being able to be creative, and the ability to provide for my family. For you, success could look different. But I can confidently say that if you are kind, likable, willing to learn, and have an interest in photography, you can do this!

It's crazy, but I have met photographers who are not kind, not good at their job, unprofessional, and they still make a living doing this. It is frustrating to run across these individuals because it's so easy to see the untapped potential that they are unwilling to access.

Whether you'd like to work part time, have a flexible schedule and make good money or carve out your own empire and put the pedal to the metal, I will go over several different possibilities.

Ultimately, the purpose of this book is to illustrate my journey of becoming a real estate photographer, what life is like in this industry, and, hopefully, to help you discover if it's what you want to do — and how to do it.

Chapter One: My First Steps

After speaking to Phil for a while, I decided to take a very large step and purchase the equipment needed to join the game. I spent close to two thousand dollars on a nice DSLR, wide angle lens, and tripod.

This was by far the biggest investment I'd ever made in anything like this, and I didn't really have the money to spare at the time. I can remember the fear I had before going to Best Buy, but I was so excited to get started that I just went for it. There was no looking back after that!

Phil taught me how to shoot HDR style photography. HDR stands for High Dynamic Range. This style is where you position your tripod in one location, take 7 to 11 exposures from that position, and then combine all of those pictures together in editing, forming one image that keeps the best exposures from all the different shots. This allows you, for example, to clearly see out the windows in a room while keeping the room as bright as possible. Once I learned this technique, I caught the bug and my interest in real estate photography went crazy!

Several agents in the office where I was already working asked me to take photos of their listings, so that's where my "on the job training" began. Prior to that, I used a point and shoot, beginner camera. Now that I had a wide-angle lens and the benefits of HDR, my shots were coming out pretty good. My angles weren't great at first. I processed the photos myself with a trial version of a processing program. I shared these photos with Phil, and he gave me tips about my angles, framing, the height of my tripod, and so on.

Phil's photos looked incredible! The lighting was perfect, he put a fire in the fireplace, a screen saver on the TVs. He could even make it sunny outside regardless of the weather in the original photo. He offered to process some of my photos for free, and when he did, I was blown away. The quality of my work suddenly became so professional. Even though I'd just started this venture, having him process for me elevated the quality of my photos to equal to or even better than competitors in the area.

Before long, I was doing shoots before work, taking very long "lunches," and shooting after work too! Anytime I shot for one of our agents they would be asked who shot their photos, which led to calls from competing agents at other offices, asking how much I charged.

Things were going so well — but there was a problem. Agents loved my quality, but I couldn't afford to send the whole job over to Phil and pay him for processing. I had so little confidence in myself, since I had just started, that I had my pricing way too low.

I felt as though I would have a difficult time starting a business on my own, so I explored working for another photographer. I met up with a local real estate photographer who had a very successful operation. He shot about 6 to 8 homes a day and needed to bring on another shooter. I shadowed him for a day and learned a ton. The issue was that he used flash photography instead of HDR. This is a completely different style and very foreign to me. But I figured if I could learn his ways, then I could work for him and make enough money to quit my regular job.

He was busy one day and asked me to do a shoot for him. I was so incredibly nervous and uncomfortable because I had no confidence shooting with a flash. Well, the shoot went horribly. The agent was very unhappy and I did not end up working with him.

The moral of the story is this:

- Find a mentor
- Never stop learning
- Have a plan
- Practice, practice, practice

Phil was my mentor. I called him every day, often several times a day. I told him about my shoots, what happened, any issues and any victories, and we would discuss them at length. We talked about interacting with the agents and the sellers — basically everything you can think of.

To this day I continue to learn and try new things. Every shoot that I go on, I learn something that helps me on my next shoot.

When I first started out, I was kind of all over the place. I knew that I loved photography in the real estate world, but I wasn't sure exactly how to start my career and what path was best. If I could start over, I would have done things differently. But I'll go into that more later.

Finally, practice is so important. Once I learned HDR photography, I went to town with it! I asked to do freebie shoots all the time, I shot my own house. I analyzed angles everywhere I went, thinking about how I would shoot this room, how I would shoot this exterior. I looked at photos on the MLS online to see what other photographers were doing. By the time I did my first paid shoot, I was so comfortable behind the camera that I was able to focus on my interaction with the client and elevating the staging and details of my shot, versus focusing on my technique and equipment.

On the flip side, when I did that single shoot for the other photographer, using the flash, I was so uncomfortable and nervous that it was a disaster from the start.

Don't ever put yourself in this position. Do not take a shoot if you are uncomfortable for any reason. In this business, the success or failure of that one shoot could mean many doors opened or closed, based on that one interaction.

Is This For Me?

If you've made it this far and still think that you would like to pursue a career in real estate photography, the next step is simple. Find a real estate photographer and ask if you can shadow them for a day. Spend the whole day with them from start to finish and watch what they do. Be sure to observe the process from the beginning to the end so you can see every detail.

How are the appointments scheduled? How do you get into the property? Who do you meet with? What product did they order? How many photos did they take? What was said to the realtor or seller? How much money was made on each shoot? Be sure to see what happens after the shoot, too. Do the photos get sent off to processing or do they process themselves?

Throughout the day, ask yourself these questions:

- Could I see myself doing this?
- What would my life look like if I did what this person is doing?
- Does it feel like a job, or fun, or hard work, or interesting?
- Based on pay, how much work would you have to do to live comfortably?

Spending this time and asking these questions will play a big part in your ability to make an informed decision. After I did this the first time, at the end of the day I was tired, overwhelmed, but incredibly excited…. I wanted in! If you don't feel that way after the first day, this may not be the path for you.

I say this because this should not just be a job, but a passion and love. It's exciting — it's a privilege to be able to do this. If you commit to it, are kind and professional, and have any sort of eye at all, you will be successful, and it will grow into something bigger than you could ever imagine. So, if you are ready to move onto the next step, let's do this!

Chapter Two: Always Be Prepared

This will be really brief, but I want to go over a few things that you will need in order to get started, as well as be prepared for everything! Sometimes it can feel like you literally live out of your car with this job, so you want to be sure that you have everything you need at all times.

First things first: you need a DSLR camera, a wide-angle lens (10mm if you have a cropped sensor, or 16mm if you have a full frame) and a tripod. We will go more in depth about gear later.

In an ideal world you will want to have a backup camera and back up lens, just in case anything happens. But when you start out, one setup will do fine.

Here's a list of other essentials:

- Backup batteries.
- An AC outlet car charger that will allow you to charge gear, your phone, and anything else you need while out on the road.
- A hot shoe mount level for your camera. Your eye is the ultimate judge of the level of your photos but having one of these is very helpful to give you a reference since you'll change positions frequently.
- An umbrella - we will discuss shooting in the rain more later, but definitely always have one of these on hand.
- Tall rain boots. Even if you are not shooting in active rain, it may have rained the day before, which can mean puddles and mud. Having these in your trunk is a HUGE advantage. One of my pet peeves is wet socks and these have saved me from this many a time.

- Spare socks. Like I said, I cannot stand having wet feet. Sometimes people have just had the carpets cleaned, so they'll be soaking, and you'll get your socks wet. It's the worst (for me at least)! Having a backup is a beautiful thing.
- Toilet paper and disinfectant. So, this is embarrassing, but it is what it is. So let's talk about it. I have been in situations where my stomach was not happy with my lunch decisions, and the use of a bathroom in a vacant home was my only choice. Since the home was vacant, there was no toilet paper….so let's just say that this is a good thing to have on hand. We will discuss this further later on.
- Hand sanitizer. I am a germaphobe, so I always sanitize after I have been in a home, which leads me to my next item.
- Gloves. I end up moving a lot of things in the homes I shoot. After the dawn of Covid-19, gloves will just be standard at every shoot. Just think about it. You touch the light switch in the bathroom, and then you think about who touched that last and if they washed their hands…eww! Another thing that gives pause for thought is a hand towel or regular towel that has been used. I move these often and they disgust me. But throw on a pair of gloves and you are good to go!
- A raincoat.
- Bug spray. Depending on where you are, bugs can get bad at certain times of the year, so this can be a real saving grace.
- Food, drinks, snacks. You can approach this however you like, but I bring a cooler with me with my lunch, snacks, and drinks. This is incredibly helpful and saves on money. I used to eat out or get drive-through several times a day, but I love the cooler so much more. It is incredibly convenient and saves me a ton of money, and allows me to be much healthier too!

- Phone charger! If I don't have this with me, I'm toast! I bought a second one specifically for my car so I always have it.
- Skateboard. Okay, I know this sounds strange, and this may not be for everyone's skill level. But sometimes when I have a shoot downtown, parking is difficult. If I have to park far away, I can board to the shoot and save a ton of time and energy. I also end up using these for shooting amenities of a neighborhood. It is annoying to pack up the tripod and camera setup, get in the car, drive a short distance, unpack it all again, and shoot, so having the board allows me to travel very easily, again saving time and energy. Disclaimer — please be careful about the safety of yourself and your equipment.

I also keep a bathing suit and towel in the trunk in case I get a break between shoots and I'm by the beach.

I said this was going to be brief…well, I guess it wasn't.

I drive about 30,000 to 35,000 miles a year and spend about 4 to 5 hours a day in the car. Most days I leave the house at 8 or 9 in the morning and get home between 6 and 10 at night. So, when I say I live out of my car, I'm not joking. Podcasts, XM radio, and streaming Netflix through my car, as well as just talking to friends and family on the phone, are things that keep me sane and help pass the time.

Which Path Is For Me?

Now begins the fun part!

If you have decided that you enjoy real estate photography, it's time to figure out what avenue you'd like to go down. Let's take a look at three different scenarios. I have done all three of them and feel that each has its advantages and disadvantages. For simplicity's sake I'm going to say that each photo shoot earns $100. I will just use estimated numbers on each process.

- A: The All-In-One - you are the boss, the processor, the scheduler, the shooter, customer service, and billing.
  - 10 minutes - scheduling
  - 30 minutes to an hour of travel
  - One hour on location shooting
  - One hour editing
  - 30 minutes delivering photos and invoicing
  - Total time invested - 3 hours and 10 minutes
  - Expenses - $0
  - Money made - $100
    - Don't forget to put aside money for taxes; check with an accountant to see what that percentage is for you and pretend like it never hit your bank account

- B: Photographer teamed up with a processor
  - 10 minutes - scheduling
  - 30 minutes to an hour of travel
  - One hour on location shooting
  - 30 minutes delivering photos and invoice
  - Total time invested - 2 hours and 10 minutes
  - Expenses - $40 for processing
  - Money made - $60
    - Don't forget to put aside money for taxes; check with an accountant to see what that percentage is and pretend like it never hit your bank account

- C: Photographer for a company
  - 0-10 minutes - scheduling - this could be done for you or done by yourself
  - 30 minutes to an hour of travel
  - One hour on location shooting
  - Expenses - $0
  - Money made - $40
    - Don't forget to put aside money for taxes; check with an accountant to see what that percentage is and pretend like it never hit your bank account

This progression is actually the exact progression that I went through. I learned tremendously at each stage. Currently, I've landed at C, but looking back I wish I had ended up at B. If I had made some adjustments, B would have been a sustainable business for me.

Remember I mentioned the importance of having a plan? I definitely did not have one going into this.

I experienced growth (and quickly, at that) but it overtook me. Before long, the business ran me versus me running a business and having any balance in my life. Honestly, it got so bad that I basically had to move in order to get away from it. So, let's go over each of these and review what's good and what's challenging with each option.

A: The All-In-One

If you know how to process photos and are good at it, this is a really good option, but it definitely presents challenges. One of the biggest issues is that you must strike a balance of being in the field and being in front of the computer editing. You will have to limit the jobs you take in order to accommodate time needed to process the photos and get them back to the clients in the expected time frame. Realtors will expect to have their photos back in a reasonable time frame, typically 48 hours. Some agents demand or expect a 24-hour turn around and even some want same day delivery! Now, if you are a good communicator and your quality is excellent, you can train your agents to expect the timeframe you need in order to deliver quality photos.

If you get really busy, your time will run out and you'll spend all night editing. Then you might find that you are running behind on your invoicing or other aspects of the business. Of course, if your pricing is appropriate, you can hire an office manager that can take care of some of these tasks for you, but you will see your bottom line get smaller. That said, I have learned there is extreme value in being able to delegate.

If this business model becomes overwhelming, another avenue to pursue is to outsource your processing. However, the biggest issue then becomes quality control. If it isn't up to snuff, you might get pushback from your clients.

I have seen photographers who chose A and ran their pics through an automated processing system. The finished product isn't super fancy, but looks good enough, and the photographer charges accordingly.

The big variable in this model is the quality of processing. You can charge more and focus on quality vs quantity, or you really run around town, burn through house after house, and deliver a mediocre or even poor-quality product. It sounds strange, but somehow even really bad "professional" photographers make a living. There are plenty of agents who are more concerned with price than quality.

B: Photographer Teamed Up With A Processor

After trying to do everything on my own, I found myself in the world of B where I sent all of my photography to an outside processor. I would shoot all day, send my pictures out at night, get them back in the next day or two. and deliver them to my clients. Processing became a large expense for me, but it was completely worth it. It bought me time, kept my product consistent, and delivered high end quality because I knew little to nothing about processing. It also allowed me to offer nice little perks to my clients, such as blue-sky replacement when it was gray or raining out. Fires could be photoshopped into the fireplaces, and screens savers placed onto the TVs. These touches really added value to my services and immediately established me as a professional even when I was just starting out.

One thing I now had to be aware of was my image count. Every shot that I submitted to processing came at a price, so I had to keep track of how many, and if my clients wanted extra photos, I had to let them know upfront about the additional cost. While I did not implement it, I would have benefited from doing an image count model, where a group of 25 images was a certain price, 40 images were this much more, and so on.

Another thing to consider with this model is that you are completely dependent on someone else. If your processor doesn't get an upload, or forgets, or goes on vacation and leaves you with no photos, you are in a tough position. Just be careful when choosing a processor. Ask a lot of questions when interviewing. Always communicate as much as possible to avoid getting your wires crossed.

All in all, this is a good path to choose because it allows you to start small and grow if you would like. You can bring on additional shooters, train them, and have the same end product because the processing is the same. Just like with plan A, if you grow and become overwhelmed, hiring an office manager to free up more time is a really good option.

C: Photographer For A Company

Due to several mistakes and poor planning on my end, I ended up in option C. I'm not saying that this is a bad option, but my method of getting to it wasn't intentional. My business got away from me, I never hired other photographers or an office manager, and I never increased my pricing. Because of these things, working for someone else seemed like an easier option than making all of those changes.

I took a pay cut in terms of my pay per job, but there were several benefits:

1. I don't have to deal with clients and complaints after the shoot
2. I always have weekends off
3. If I go on vacation, I have others on the team who will cover for me
4. If I get sick, others can cover for me

5. All of my appointments are scheduled for me

In going from business owner/shooter/admin/bill collector to just shooter for someone else, my overall stress went down, and actually my overall pay did go up. With all of these options, the money has been really good (better than I ever could have imagined) and there have been a ton of perks. It's just a matter of considering what route you'd like to go. I definitely suggest having a plan.

Speaking of perks, let's talk about some!

Chapter Three: Let's Talk About The Perks

I'm thrilled to have a job that allows me to be creative, one that lets me use my ten years of experience in the field — but one of the biggest allures to pursuing this path is the money.

When I started looking at the money involved in doing just a couple shoots a day, I quickly figured out that I could make more in a day than I did in a week at my other job. It's incredibly exciting to be able to do something that you enjoy and be nicely rewarded for it.

I always struggled with having to be in a 9-5 job. It felt like a prison to me. While being a photographer isn't just a case of, "Do whatever you want," it is much more flexible. I have found that as long as I communicate with my agents and clients, I have some freedom with my time. I can fit in doctor's appointments, have family time, sleep in, or other things while still getting my work done. My schedule has been far more fluid, and that fits my personality much more than a rigid "you have to be here now or else" type of schedule.

I have been able to see and experience some incredible things over the years. You get to see how the top 1% lives (as well as the bottom 1%) and they are usually pretty excited to show off to you. I have seen a bowling alley in someone's basement, breathtaking infinity pools that overlook the ocean, penthouses with crazy views, celebrity homes, backyards that cost more than what I consider really nice homes, a helipad on a roof, safe rooms, and so much more. Homeowners have taken me out on their boats to get the perfect shot, and many kind homeowners and agents have treated me to really nice meals over the years.

I meet these sellers at a time when they are moving and often downsizing. So, it's a great opportunity to purchase some nice items, or even come across some free things. I have been given some nice stuff over the years, as well as just asking if they're looking to sell things that I'm interested in as we go through the house.

You will meet some of the nicest and some of the craziest people you could ever imagine doing this. If you enjoy talking, there are many stories you will hear — sometimes whether you want to or not!

I'm not sure if I'd consider this next one a perk, but it is something cool I'd like to mention. This will sound completely off topic but stay with me. Have you ever played Grand Theft Auto? I did a long, long time ago, probably the first one that ever came out, and that was the end of that. I bring it up because there was a really neat feature in the game where it tabulated all of your statistics: how many steps you've taken, minutes played, workouts completed, etc. Anyways, I've always thought that God has a specific book for me with all my stats — hours slept, pounds of McDonalds consumed, money spent on baseball cards, everything. In my life I have spent hundreds of hours and thousands of dollars on music, whether learning how to play and compose, recording, being in a band. I have posted video after video on YouTube trying to share my music with the world, and it has gone nowhere. The most views I have on YouTube is around 100.

But I got into this real estate photography thing with no experience, no schooling, and very little investment. I wish I could call upon the universe for the official stats, but I would argue that my photos have been seen several million times. While no one knows that they were my work, I'm still amazed to think that what I do has such a huge impact on my clients, the sellers, and potential buyers. Just thinking about that helps me realize that what I do has a purpose and fuels me to want to continue, rather than it just being a job that I get paid to do.

I don't want to dedicate a whole chapter to the downsides or difficulties of real estate photography. But I do want you to have the whole picture, so you know what you are getting yourself into.

The first aspect was number one for perks, too — money. Real estate photography is cyclical, and this is something you must be aware of and plan for. As you are growing, you won't have past years to review activity and predict patterns, but as you continue, this data will help you to plan your schedule. I have found that the time from Thanksgiving to New Year's dips a ton. Sometimes work dips in the summer as well, when people go on vacation.

It is different in different climates. When I shot in New Jersey, Thanksgiving until about mid-February was super slow due to the snow and difficult weather. When I lived in Florida, the winter gap was not as large because of the nice weather year-round. Be prepared for this. As you are starting out, I recommend having another form of income that will allow you to grow your business and take appointments.

Another aspect you need to think of is weather. This is out of your control but has a large impact on how much you can shoot. There have been several weeks where I was unable to work, due to snowstorms, hurricanes, and other natural disasters. The point is just to be prepared. As Dave Ramsey advises, have an emergency fund. I strongly recommend having 3 to 6 months of savings available as soon as possible so when these times hit — and they will hit — you are not scrambling and stressed about finances. In fact, when these times come about, you can actually really enjoy the time off.

While those examples are extreme, there's also just the very frequent occurrence of rain. On rainy days, I tell agents that I can go ahead and shoot and do a blue-sky replacement so no one will ever know that the weather was inclement. Sometimes the timeframe is so urgent that the agents and sellers really want it to be shot on that day. I've often encouraged them to keep their appointment because rescheduling is complicated. But now I am at a point where bad weather really does negatively affect the shoot, and I am happy to reschedule and not be out in the rain with my boots and umbrella.

There is a ton of driving, as mentioned before. Sometimes it can be lonely. There are negative things, just like in any job — but there have been so many times where I literally want to pinch myself because I can't believe I get paid to be in such beautiful places and see such amazing sights.

When I think back to my 9-5 job or being a realtor and working my butt off and not even getting paid for it, I can't believe that what I do exists and that I'm fortunate enough to be doing it.

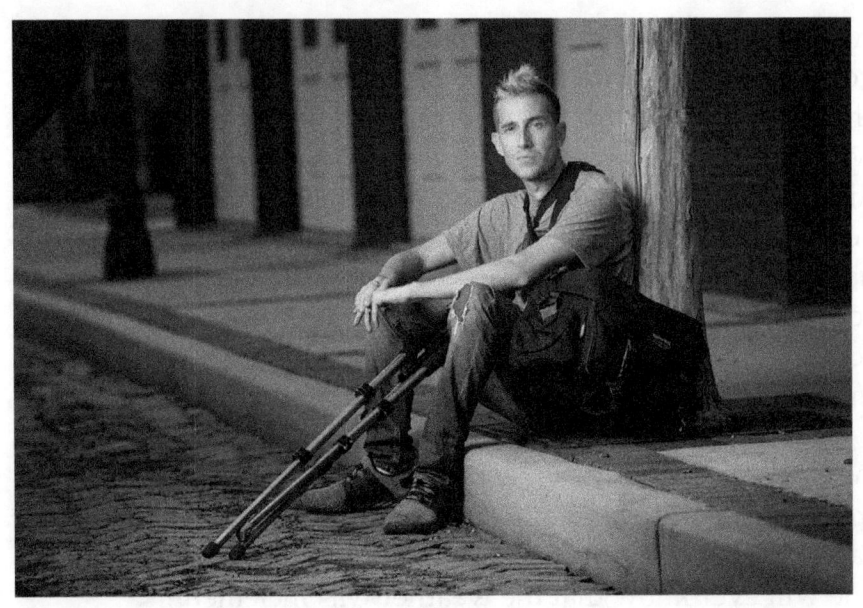

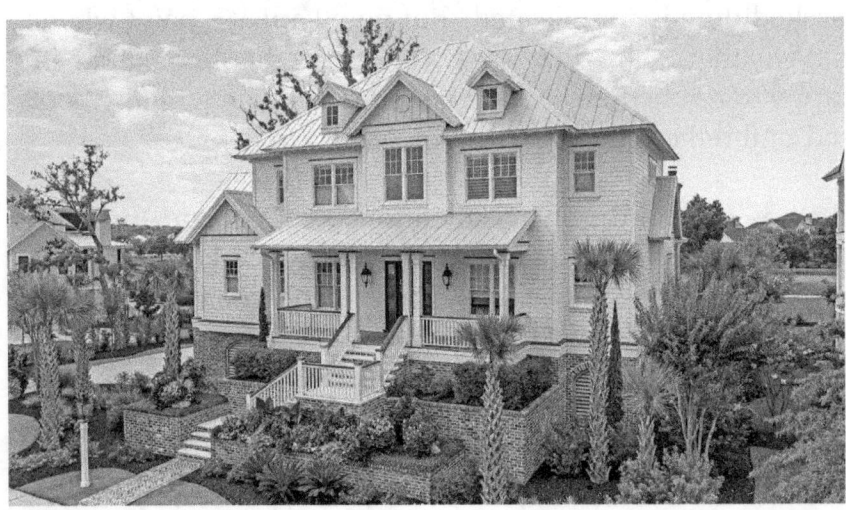

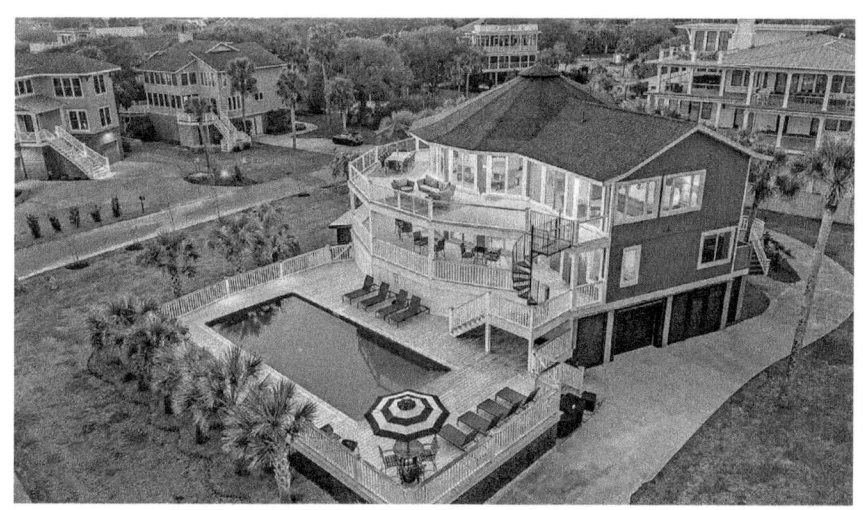

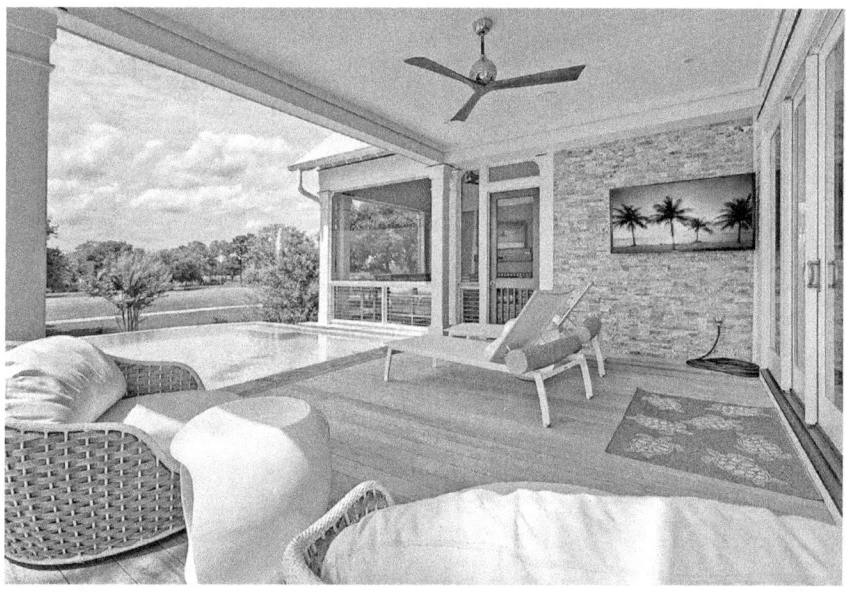

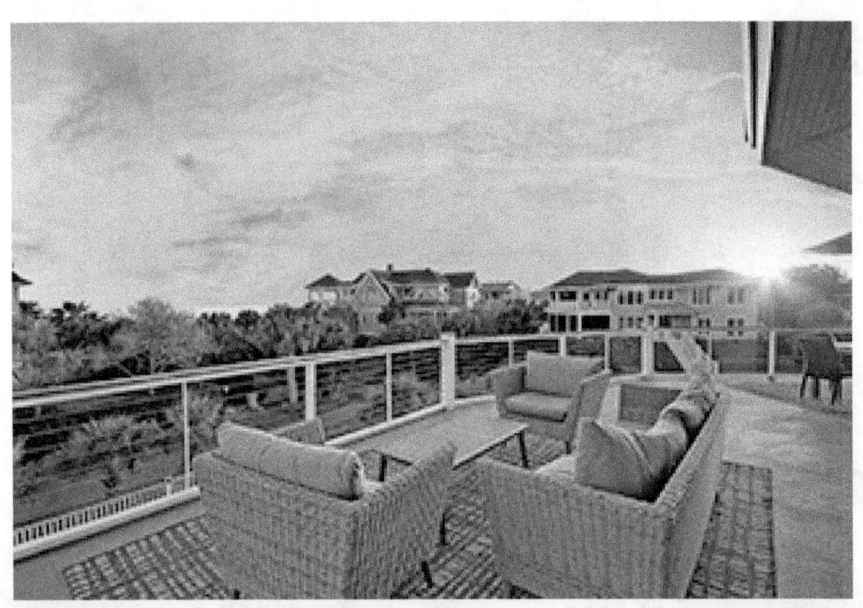

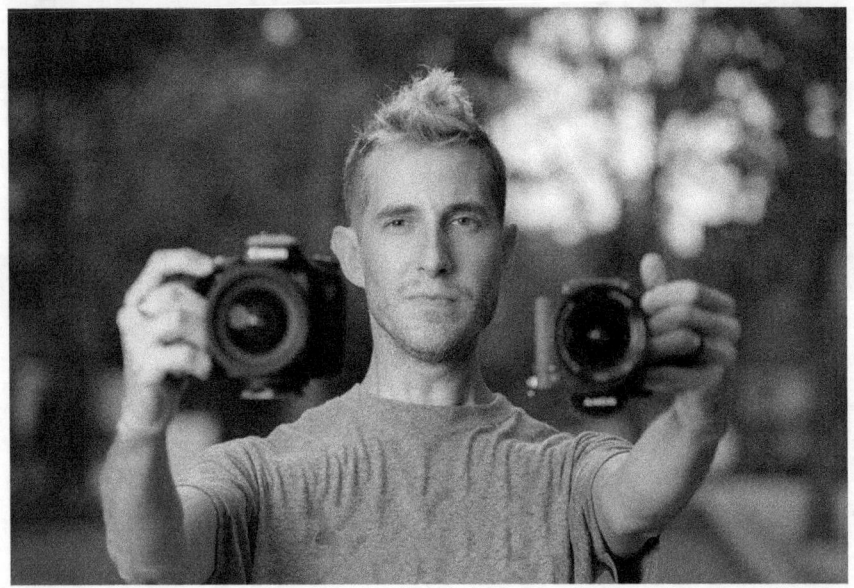

Chapter Four: **Getting Started**

Now that you have a path…what next?

Let's work backwards with this one. If you are going with plan C and working with a photography company, it's time to start looking around to find a company where you will be a good fit. To do this, simply do a Google search to find some of the bigger companies out there. You can also track down some realtors and see who they use.

This can be a good way to go about it as well because it might help you find a single photographer who is doing well and potentially looking to expand. If the two of you get along, this is a great chance to get started with a mentor who will be completely invested in your success.

Some good questions to ask are:

- What is the compensation?
- Is there any room for growth?
- Is training provided?
- Do you provide any equipment?
- Who does the scheduling?
- Who does the processing?
- What different products do you offer?

These are just a few to get the ball rolling, but ultimately the most important thing is whether you get along with the people at the company. If it is a company with several shooters, talk to the other shooters and see what they have to say. That will be the best way to gauge what it will be like to work there.

If you choose path A or B, things are a little more difficult. There's no one guaranteed way to make it work for you. Honestly, you could do almost everything right and your business still might just not take off.

I'd like to share what I have witnessed be successful in three different markets.

First off, it takes time to grow. You need a good product at the right price and the ability to build relationships with realtors, because that is the key to your success. (More on that later). During this time, please have another form of income so that you can build your business the right way, not in a financial rush.

The best way to grow your business is to get your work out there. You usually need to do this for free at first, but it is worth it. A realtor will use you, they will post to the MLS, and then hundreds and possibly thousands of realtors will see your work. Realtors talk…they are really good at it. I have witnessed many agents in an office environment, making flyers or posting to MLS, asking each other, "Who did your photos?" The next question will be, "How much was it?" Hopefully, all the talk about how professional, knowledgeable, and nice you were, as well as the quality of the photos, will lead to your first paying gig.

Photographic Philosophy

Yes, I am a photographer, but more importantly, I am a real estate photographer. I have to think like a real estate agent. My goal when I go into a home aligns with that of the agent and the homeowner: to sell that home for the most money possible in the least amount of time.

Once an agent knows that I share this same goal, we really become a team. I can't stress enough the importance of building relationships with agents. I can train the agent on how best to prep his/her homes and his/her sellers for photography. If they aren't using a stager, I can coach them on tips and tricks for de-cluttering, making rooms look bigger and brighter, and how to coordinate the timing of photography to work out perfectly with their goal date to list the home. As trust builds and the relationship grows, it often will progress from the agents and sellers being there to "hold your hand" for the shoot, to the agent just trusting you to get the job done.. They know that anything I say to their seller will be in line with what they want — to get the home sold!

One of my favorite sayings is, "People don't care how much you know until they know how much you care." I love this and it is so true! The majority of my clients bought into me before they bought into my photography. When I offer a free shoot after meeting them, I go all out and do everything I can to make their property shine and to make sure their seller has a positive experience. I also recommend anything that I can offer which might help them in their marketing. If I run into a really special property which needs something extra to really make it pop and they don't want to pay for it, I'll just go ahead and do it.

Prior to working with agents, I always ask questions about the agent, about their business, about their successes, and most importantly about their family and their interests. Another thing I do is follow up with my agents a few weeks later with a text or a call. "Hey, just wanted to see how 123 Main Street is doing."

Or, when I see them at the next listing, I'll always follow up about the last one we were at together.

It just shows that I care about them. I remember what we do together. My interest in them shows that it's more than just a job to me.

Difficult Conversations

There are a few conversations that I find myself having with agents and homeowners over and over again. Here are some that you should know about and be prepared for.
"It's not you, it's me." Thanks to HGTV and other programming like it, the awareness of what to do when selling is much higher than it was when I first started. But there are still plenty of people out there who have no clue what to do before listing their home. If I am at a "hands on" photo shoot where the agent wants me to double as a stager, I will basically hide all of the owner's personal effects, decorations, and knick-knacks. These items, especially photos or sentimental things, can be very personal, so this is the basic script that I go with to avoid offending anyone. "I love this _____ and what you have done in the _____, but in order to appeal to the largest pool of buyers, it helps to remove anything that might distract viewers from seeing your space for what it is and imagining themselves in it."

In an ideal world, the owner leaves those items hidden. It's up to the agent to coach them on this. If I get any pushback, I assure them that I'll put everything back as I found it once I am done. And if I get a ton of pushback, then we shoot as is, and it is what it is. Assuring the sellers that removing these personal things is an important part of selling the home quickly and for top dollar usually has a lot of power. But there will definitely be times when you'll just be unable to convince Bertha of the importance of moving the giant decorative cow from the center island in the kitchen.

"It's cloudy out! "- One thing I highly recommend is being able to offer blue sky replacement during processing. This allows you to work even when it's cloudy out or raining. I've even shot in the snow before. If they're still uneasy with this option, show them before and after pictures of the process. You might also point out that the timeline is very important. If the house needs to be on the market by Friday and it's Wednesday now, the shoot needs to happen, and the seller can trust in the quality of processing.

I easily handle the whole cloudy objection with this. "I actually love it when it's cloudy out, because I don't have to compete with the sun, and everything ends up being evenly lit." Most times, this does the trick, but I must be honest with you about this situation. I used to be convinced that every agent and seller should keep the appointment, no matter what the weather conditions were. However, the more I do this, the more I just want what the agent wants.

If timeframe is more important than quality, then I'm happy to shoot it. If they need the listing to be the absolute best and it's so cloudy and dark out that I know it will drastically negatively affect the quality of the photos and listings, I'm happy to reschedule.

Ultimately, we are only as good as the quality of our last shoot. So if we say, "It'll be fine," and it isn't, that makes us look bad, it makes the agent look bad, it makes the photos look bad, and the whole situation could really affect future business for us and that client.

My personal take away on this topic:

- If the timeline is most important, no matter what, let's do it!
- If the quality is most important, let's reschedule!
- If you are unsure at all whether they will be unhappy, let the agent make the call.

"3 PM is the only time we can shoot this house; the lighting is perfect." - Easy short answer: "While 3 PM may be perfect for the front, it might not be the best time for the rest of the home; in fact, it might be a horrible time for the backyard. We can keep our appointment for tomorrow afternoon and be flexible, or if it must be exactly at 3, my next availability is next week."

I really want to prevent the agent believing that homes can only be shot a certain time, because it will result in a scheduling nightmare moving forward. It also creates the illusion that homes can only be shot at certain times, and that's simply not true, especially with editing. My personal take is that if I have a really important shoot or especially a video, I try to shoot it close to noon. I find that's the most evenly lit time of day. But again, I don't let the agents know this, because then they will only want to book me for noon.

"To hide or not to hide." -Sometimes, agents and sellers just assume, "Oh we can just photoshop that out." Usually, technically speaking, the answer is yes, we can. But depending on what "that" is, the answer is definitely not always yes. I have been asked if I could erase both of the neighbors' houses out of the shot. I have been asked if I could remove a small public electrical box in the front yard. I have been asked if I can erase giant electrical power lines in the backyard.

When asked this question, I respond with this question. "Will it be there when someone comes to see the house?" If the answer is yes, then my answer is no.

I have been asked if I could finish "painting" a room. I have been asked if I could fix a crack in the wall. I have been asked if I can patch up dirt with grass in the yard. If they assure me that they are going to be making that repair and I believe them, then yes, we can perform that edit for them comfortably.

Now, that being said, there are also ways to be creative with angles to work around some of these things. I can crop in tight so the neighbors' houses are not easily seen. I can stand in front of the electrical box in the front yard, so I don't bring attention to it. I do not find this deceitful; it's just painting the picture in the best light.

One common conversation is the seller not wanting to open the blinds because they don't want people to see how close it is to the other homes. While I understand this, I do not feel that you should ever deliberately hide something from potential buyers. You may get more showings on your listing, but those people will immediately be turned off upon discovering the thing that was hidden. They will feel deceived and not be interested any longer. However, if you paint an accurate picture in the photos, viewers will be fully informed before scheduling a showing, and thus more serious and educated. The goal, again, is to sell the home, not to just get showings. I understand that views lead to showings and showings lead to offers, but I strongly feel that showing potential buyers the full story is the way to go.

"Poor planning on your end does not constitute an emergency on my end." - This is another of my favorite sayings, and it is so applicable to this job and industry. In general, real estate agents need something done and they need it done yesterday. Knowing this as you build your relationships with agents, you can train them on your photo processing process. If it takes two business days to process the photos, be sure to communicate that to the agent upfront in the beginning. When they are scheduling the appointment, go ahead and ask them right there.

Agent: I'd like to book you for Thursday
Me: Okay, great! When are you looking to list this house?
Agent: Friday
Me: Okay, if we shoot on Thursday, I might get them back on Friday, but honestly, I can't guarantee it. Can we schedule on Wednesday, or are you and your sellers flexible with your list date?

If you have this conversation up front, there will be no confusion. I can't tell you how many times this has happened to me.

Prep your agents so they can properly prep their sellers. Another saying I love is, "Don't over-promise and under-deliver. Over-deliver and under-promise." My good agents will do something like this. They'll schedule me on a Monday, knowing that they will have their photos back by Wednesday; however, they will tell the sellers they won't get them back until Friday. This way, they stay ahead of the curve and have much more control over the situation. Which leads me to my next point: control.

Control The Situation

Over time, you will begin to be a master of ceremonies. You will learn to train your agents. You will learn to guide your sellers, and YOU will call the shots. If you are not innately confident or authoritative, time and experience in this job will enable you to be a strong leader for your agents and sellers.

I am a shy guy and have struggled with confidence throughout my life. I submit to authority and have difficulty saying no. However, in my role as a real estate photographer, I am the leader and I make the rules. For example, sometimes I will enter a home and be introduced to the seller who offers to give me a tour of the home. I respectfully decline and say that I will be shooting the whole home, so I'll see everything then, but if there are any hidden rooms or doors, please let me know.

I have always looked younger than I actually am. When I was 30, everyone thought I was in high school. Sellers and agents have often asked me, "How old are you?" It amuses me that my potential young age would affect my ability to photograph their home, but when dealing with multi-million-dollar homes I do understand their concern. I just assure them that I am skilled at my craft and excited to photograph their home.

One common situation that I run across is the home that is not ready, where the sellers or agents just think, "Oh, we'll just move things from room to room." What they don't realize is that they and their things are going to be in the way all the time, so it is up to me to take control and make it as easy as possible on everyone. One way that I've found works well is to assess the situation when you first arrive in the home. Sometimes it's such a mess that you just need to reschedule. Sometimes, it's obvious that the mess isn't going anywhere, so you have to shoot it as it is. However, many times it just needs a little work and direction from you to get 'er done!

One great trick is to go in the home with the agent and seller. Tell them, "I'm going to shoot the 2nd and 3rd bedroom and the laundry room now. Then I'm going to go outside and shoot the exteriors to give you time to stash everything in those rooms while I'm outside. That way we only have to move things once and it will be easiest to get the rest of the home."

The important thing to remember is that as a real estate photographer I shoot homes every day; however, a seller only sells their home once every four years, or even once every forty years. So it's up to me to help them.

Stay Safe And CYA

There are definitely several things that I want to recommend in order for you to stay safe in this job.

The first thing is to always announce yourself when entering a "vacant" home. Often, my order will say the home I am going to is vacant, but then I will show up, use the lockbox, open the door, and see there is someone standing in front of me. Prior to entering a home, I ring the doorbell and knock, and then upon entering I will say very loudly, "Hello! Photographer!" just to let anyone know that I am there.

There have been several occasions where someone is in the bathroom or shower and they had no clue I was coming, so it is very important to alert them to your presence.

Although this has not happened to me personally, I am always careful to announce myself to prevent being shot by someone who thinks I am trespassing. I have had a shotgun pulled on me twice. Both happened when I was taking photos of vacant land. When you are in remote locations like this, despite having a gigantic tripod and camera, you'll still be questioned, "What are you doing here?"

Part of me really wants to respond that I am there to steal all the blades of grass and sell them on the black market but being greeted by the end of a barrel is definitely a scary thing.

The easiest way to prevent a situation like this is to have the realtor accompany you to the shoot. I love not having the realtor with me, normally, since it just makes life so easy. But for the situation of vacant land in rural areas, it is helpful to have them with you not only for protection but also to point out the bounds of the property. If they do not accompany you, definitely speak with them on the phone to ensure you know the boundaries of the property (have them send you a tax map). Also have them give you the name of the owner of the property, so if you are confronted by Jim Bob Earl the neighbor, you can tell them that Mr. Smith is selling the land and asked you to take photos for him. Rural areas are usually tight knit communities, so dropping the name that they are familiar with is like a free pass.

When it comes to vacant homes, you really want to exercise caution. If you are nervous about a dangerous neighborhood and a vacant home, be sure to tell someone the address that you are going to and when you will be there and call them when you are done. If you are unable to bring someone with you, this is the next best thing. I often speak to friends throughout the day to help pass the time. If you are able to chat with someone while in that vacant home, that's an extra level of protection because they'll "be there" with you. Of course, if you ever don't feel comfortable, then do not take the job. It's definitely not worth it. Or just be sure to ask the agent to accompany you!

As I walk through a property, there are several things that I do.

1). I am always looking at the ground to avoid stepping in dog poop. Dog poop is everywhere but if you always watch where you are going. this will minimize the number of bombs you step on.

2) I also am always searching the ground for snakes. I have run into snakes several times. Creating a rustling noise makes them slither away, but I am just always on the lookout for them as well.

3). I HATE SPIDERS!!!! In order to reduce my exposure to them, I walk with my tripod extended out in front of me so that it hits the webs before my face does. On one of my first shoots on Kiawah Island in South Carolina, I saw a banana spider in a web in the backyard. Apparently, these beasts are friendly, but if you have never seen one before and come across one…it is terrifying! I enjoy seeing them now but the first time, I screamed loudly and jumped up and down for a long time.

A second way that my tripod has protected me from physiological and physical harm is from attacking dogs. There have been many times where no one told me an attack dog was on the property or in the fenced-in backyard. As they charged me, I pointed my fully extended tripod at them, and it created a wonderful barrier between me and the bloodthirsty animal. All of this sounds crazy, I know, but it's for real!

Now in terms of CYA (cover your ass) tactics, I have a few of those.

The first is just a personal practice that you may not experience but which I have found helpful. There are many times when I leave a property and think to myself, "Did I lock the door? Did I turn the lights off?" I will actually turn back and double check myself to make sure that I left the property the way I found it.

In order to prevent having to do this, as I close up the property, I will say out loud, "Lights are off!" When I put the key back in the lockbox, I will say out loud to myself, "Key is in the box!" And then I will say, "Doors are locked!" out loud as I lock all the doors. If I am particularly nervous about something, I will take a picture with my phone to prove to myself and anyone else that it was that way when I left.

I have two stories that I'd like to share to show that purchasing insurance for yourself is a super smart thing to do.

Story one: I was taking photos of an old home in New Jersey in the winter. When I got to the basement, there was a room with the door closed. I opened it, took a photo of the room, and moved on. A few days later I received a phone call from the realtor, expecting them to say they sold the home and how grateful they were for the photography. However, the conversation went a little bit differently. She explained that the pipes burst in the basement, which resulted in the home flooding — and it happened because I left that door open in the basement. Now, no one ever told me that it needed to stay closed. If the home was being shown, this could have easily been done by a fellow realtor or buyer. But the fact was that there was extensive damage to the home, and they were looking for someone to blame for it. The realtor asked if I had insurance, I said no, and luckily it just sort of went away. But it was a horrible feeling, especially since I was very close with the realtor, and I felt like they were really grasping at straws with that one.

Story two: I arrived at a property for a twilight shoot and walked up to meet the homeowner who was on a ladder changing a lightbulb on the outside of his garage. I didn't want to startle him, but when I said, "Hi there!" — well, I startled him. The poor guy dropped the lightbulb, knocked over the ladder, and fell on his butt so hard! I couldn't believe what I had just seen. I called 911 and asked him if I could do anything. He broke both of his arms and both of his legs. Witnessing this was extremely disturbing, but even worse, I felt responsible. Even though it really wasn't my fault, I felt completely guilty about the situation. Thank God he was one of the nicest guys ever and nothing ever came of it, but I was terrified he might claim it was my fault and I would be responsible for insane medical bills and much more. I purchased insurance the next day!

Something else I wanted to mention in this section is to really be careful what you do and what you say, because these days you can almost count on being recorded in many of the homes you enter. Many years ago, it was only in multi-million-dollar homes, and the agent would warn me as we went on the property that we were being constantly monitored. Today, this is really the case in every price range. With the Ring doorbell and other systems so readily available, visual and audio monitoring is super common. Be aware of what you say, maybe if you are on the phone or if you are in the home with the realtor, there is a very big chance the homeowners are somewhere else listening.

This has turned into quite a lengthy section, but it is really important to be careful and always protect yourself. Being in others' homes is a liability. Anything can happen, even things you'd never expect or imagine, so it's best to be prepared!

Chapter Five: It's Not Just Photos

I didn't mention this in perks, but this is definitely one of them. Having this job is not just about taking photographs. I mean, it can be, but there are opportunities for much more. You will run into a ton of different people, which can lead to all sorts of different things. The most common question I am asked is, "Do you do weddings?" Now, I don't, but if you do, that's a huge opportunity. I also don't do head shots, but that is another one that I am asked all the time.

Another opportunity that I ran into was writing the descriptions for real estate listings on the MLS. I do not think that I am good at writing these, but many agents have asked me to do this, and it has become a good source of extra income.

Over the years I have met executives, politicians, inventors, musicians, celebrities, and of course a ton of agents. Not only is it just fun and extremely interesting, but you just never know where it's going to lead!

Besides the standard real estate photo shoot, the marketing of a property today can involve so much more than photos. Between video, aerials, twilights, and 3D video there are a ton of different products that you can offer to your clients. Let's go over these.

The easiest add-on to introduce to your repertoire is twilights. A twilight photo shoot is where you go back to the property at sundown, open all the blinds, and turn on all the lights inside and outside. The glow from the lights inside and outside combined with the sunset or darkened sky in the background creates an amazing photo. Twilights attract more attention and clicks online and have an emotional component to them which connects with viewers. The going rate for twilights is very good, so adding these is a huge way to increase your income.

Video is becoming more and more popular. Depending on your skill level, you can charge anywhere from $100 to thousands of dollars. Remember how I mentioned I knew nothing about cameras before starting this? Well, I knew even less about video, but I have the privilege of knowing two people who are experts with a video camera. I asked both of them if they ever needed help with their jobs and offered to be a PA (production assistant) for them. While working with them, I just observed everything I could. I asked a ton of questions and soaked up all that was said and done during the shoots. I learned enough about lighting, sound, cameras, and editing during this time to be dangerous enough to offer realtors a quality video product.

I want to take a moment to thank and express my gratitude to Jason from Awakened Films and Alex from VideoTrekker Films for being such a huge part of my growth in terms of working with video. Their friendship, advice, expertise and knowledge of their craft played a huge role in my development. Having people like this in your life is invaluable.

When DJI introduced the first Phantom, I immediately bought one. I knew this invention would change the way real estate photography was done. Since then, it has become more and more popular, and it's a tool that I use all the time. It is quite expensive, and to do it correctly and legally you need to get licensed and insured, but it is definitely worth it. Drone photography is another great way to market certain properties and it definitely helps attract attention to listings online.

One of the newest additions to real estate marketing is 3D virtual tours through Matterport or Zillow 3D tours. This is a great way for agents to virtually show homes and is becoming more and more popular.

I could go on and on about each one of these things, but the point is, the more products you can offer, the more money you can make. Some days I'll have six regular photo jobs, and other days I'll have just one or two jobs that have several products each resulting in even more money than the six regular jobs.

What To Shoot

I could go over exactly what I shoot on my appointments, but since everyone's business and every home is different, I'd like to just go over some basic guidelines. It will depend on what type of business model you are working with (like whether you are shooting a 25-image package, etc.), but essentially, you want to shoot the whole house.

- A few of the front; be sure to provide a few variations of the front as this is usually their cover shot
- Six or eight of the backyard

- Treat outdoor living spaces as a room in a home, such as front porches, screened-in porches, patios, etc.
- One or two of the foyer
- One or two of the living room, dining room, three of the family room, at least three of the kitchen (if not more)
- Two or more of the master bedrooms
- Two or more of the master bathroom
- One of secondary bedrooms and baths
- Garage - typically, don't take pictures of this unless there are nice built-ins, man-cave, workshop, etc.

It's always best to CYA and shoot everything. When you get home, review your shots and only send the best. Then, if the agent comes back and says, "Oh, did you take a shot of _____?" Hopefully you will have it and working this way will help you not send the agent too much, letting you just pick out the best for them.

How To Shoot

This is another topic that I could go on about for days, but I want to go over a few guidelines and rules — although they aren't really rules because there's always opportunities to break them. To be honest about this subject, there is no ONE way to shoot; angles and composition are subjective, but I have found some common rules that I follow, and which seem to work.

Shooting from the corners of rooms and straight-ons are usually the best angles. Anything in between a corner angle and a straight-on ends up looking strange.

Don't shoot looking up or down. There are opportunities to break this rule, but they are rare occasions.

Landscape, as opposed to portrait, is almost always the preferred orientation. Sometimes you can break this when you need height, like in a two -story foyer, walk-in shower, or two-story family room with a fireplace. I recommend taking both a landscape and portrait of these angles and reviewing them when you get home.

Always pull focus with something in the back of the frame so everything is in focus and you don't create depth of field.

In terms of framing, always think of what is in the absolute center of the frame, what is anchoring the right, and what is anchoring the left. Oftentimes the corner of a room, the ceiling fan/light, or a piece of furniture ends up being in the center of the frame and making a nice shot. Sometimes you will have to choose between framing for a room or framing for the furniture. If you are not sure, shoot both and review at home.

In terms of furniture try not to shoot the back of a couch or a chair. If it's a couch, make sure you're higher than its level with your tripod or just take a few steps forward and shoot over it. If it's the back of a chair, turn it so it opens to your frame for a more inviting shot.

In terms of camera height, always be above counter tops and furniture.

Let the wide-angle lens go to work for you and make everything as big as possible. We are selling space, so the more we can show (most of the time) the better! It's amazing what taking one step backwards will do in terms of opening up a room. Also, just a slight tweak to the left or the right can make a world of difference. I suggest doing those things before you finalize your framing and start shooting.

Follow your gut! Sometimes a shot will just feel right! Other times, it simply won't feel right. When it doesn't feel right, just keep on shooting until it does. If it never does, just shoot a ton and then when you get home and review you'll find that one of the angles, or several, look good on the computer. It's very strange, but sometimes I review angles on my camera in the field and I'm not in love with the shot, but when I get home, they look much better.

You Are Worth It

I mentioned some mistakes I made earlier on that I wanted to revisit. When I was looking to grow my business, I got impatient and wanted things to grow faster than they were. There was a top producer who I knew, and I was really going after her to earn her business. Since I basically had no business at that point, I was willing to do anything.

The two mistakes that I made were offering her a price that was WAY too low and allowing her to stage her listings for the photos while I was there instead of them being ready to be shot when I arrived. In hindsight, I should have offered that amazing price only for a limited time, like a year or six months, and then raised it from there. And since I didn't have enough confidence in myself, or because I was just afraid of her going somewhere else, I didn't realize that I should have charged her a staging fee or told her the properties needed to be ready when I arrived.

Be sure to charge a fee if you travel over a certain mile range from your home.

Be sure to charge a fee if they want you to come back "just to take a couple."

Be sure to charge if the client cancels for no reason at all. You blocked off time for them and that prevented you from making money with someone else.

Be sure to charge for anything that is above and beyond your normal services.

I know this section sounds greedy, but it is super important to implement in the beginning. If you try to add fees and things like that after you've established clients, it doesn't go very well. Another thing I want to add about these fees is that if you have them in place, it then gives you leverage to waive the fee or provide incentives. I am all about offering things for free or going above and beyond for clients. It's something I LOVE doing and I feel it reaps rewards down the road. These are some ways to position this in a variety of different arenas.

"We do have a $_____ travel fee to go to _____ but if you are able to schedule 2 or 3 in one day, I'm happy to waive that."

"Typically, we do have a $_____ cancellation fee but I'm happy to waive this for you since it's your first time."

"I know it took us a while to get this one just right with the extra on-site staging. We actually do offer a $_____ staging consult. If you ever run into another one of these in the future, just be sure to let me know so I can schedule in the extra time beforehand. I'm happy to waive the fee this time, these are going to turn out so nice."

Just a quick note on this one: if you ever run into one of these, be sure to take before photos with your phone of each room you stage. After you process your photos you can present the before and after pics to the agent as a wonderful listing presentation that they can use, too. Explain that most agents won't do any staging and will just use their phones to take the pictures and then show what your pics and the staging looks like. This is an incredibly powerful tool that you just gave the agent and one of those gestures that will really show the agent 1) how much you care and 2) how valuable you are to their business!

"I know you didn't order aerial photos, but I just really felt like this was a wonderful home to be showcased from above and provided some for free. Typically, this service is $_____." This is a wonderful way for an agent to try out a service for free and the chances of them using it in the future are very high. Even if they don't, you just scored brownie points and showed them that you love what you do and care about what they do.

The point is, you start out with not much to do, but over time you end up in high demand. Just know from the start that you are worth it, and your time is very valuable. The more you do this, the more you will see what an impact you have on so many different things.

I started out by saying that I met another Phil and it changed my life. I would like to be that Phil for you.

If you've read through all this craziness and you're looking to find out more, I want to hear from you. I'd love to chat, hear where you are at, and answer any questions you might have.

About The Author

Phil Johnson is a Christian and loves God.

He is a son to Perry and Helen and grateful for all that they have taught him. They have always encouraged him to pursue his passions.

He is a brother to Julie, Perry, Peter, Tony, Felicia, Joe and Tim. His siblings are incredibly supportive and amazing humans.

He is a husband to his wife Aly who has been by his side through all the ups and downs of this journey.

He is a father to Elijah, the most amazing son a dad could ask for.

Last but not least, he is a real estate photographer who is so excited to share his journey and experiences with anyone who is looking to learn more about this crazy, exciting and unique career path.

Please feel free to contact me if you have any questions at phildanieljohnson@yahoo.com.